THE HISTORY DETECTIVE

INVESTIGATES

Roman Britain

Peter Hepplewhite

WAYLAND

The History Detective Investigates series:
Anglo-Saxons
The Celts
The Civil Wars
The Industrial Revolution
Local History
Post-War Britain
Roman Britain
Tudor Exploration
Tudor Home
Tudor Medicine
Tudor Theatre
Tudor War
Victorian Crime
Victorian Factory
Victorian School
Victorian Transport

First published in Great Britain in 2006 by Wayland,
an imprint of Hachette Children's Books

© Copyright 2006 Hodder Wayland

Reprinted in 2007 by Wayland,
an imprint of Hachette Children's Book

This paperback edition published in 2008 by Wayland, an imprint of
Hachette Children's Books, 338 Euston Road, London NW1 3BH
www.hachettelivre.co.uk

Editor: Hayley Leach
Designer: Simon Borrough
Cartoon artwork: Richard Hook
Maps and diagrams: Peter Bull

British Library Cataloguing in Publication Data

Roman Britain. - (The history detective investigates)
    1.Romans - Great Britain - Social life and customs -
    Juvenile literature 2.Great Britain - History - Roman
    period, 55 B.C. -449 A.D. - Juvenile literature
    I.Title
    936.1'04

ISBN: 978-0-7502-5611-7

Printed and bound in China

The publishers would like to thank the
following for permission to reproduce their
pictures:
akg-images/Erich Lessing 14, 16, 20; The Art
Archive/Museo Capitolino Rome/Dagli Orti
4; Butser Ancient Farm 18 and 19; Dorset
County Museum, UK/Bridgeman Art Library
20; R. Embleton 17; Robert Estall/Corbis 13;
Jason Hawkes/Corbis 25; Museum of
Antiquities, Newcastle 23; TopFoto.co.uk
Collection Roger-Viollet 5; TopFoto.co.uk
cover, 7, 12 and title page, 16, 21, 26, 29, 28;
TopFoto.co.uk Museum of London 8-9, 11,
27 (top); TopFoto.co.uk The British Museum
24, 25, 27 (bottom); Wayland Picture Library
Jim Kershaw 22 (left), The British Museum
22 (right).

Contents

Words in **bold** can be found in the glossary on page 30

The history detective Sherlock Bones, will help you to find clues and collect evidence about Roman Britain. Wherever you see one of Sherlock's paw-prints, you will find a mystery to solve. The answers can be found on page 31.

1. Who were the Romans?

When the Romans invaded in AD 43 British tribes had little chance of defending their land against them. Roman armies were highly trained, well led and hardly ever lost a battle. Britain was about to become part of the mighty Roman Empire – whether the British liked it or not. Yet, the Romans had not always been so powerful. Their climb to greatness took many centuries.

The early Romans were farmers who lived on seven hills in a region called Latium, in what is now Italy. Little is known about their early history but, according to legend, the city of Rome was founded in 753 BC. At first the Romans only ruled the area around Rome but by 270 BC they had defeated neighbouring tribes and taken over the whole of Italy. And this was just the beginning! By AD 130 Roman armies had **conquered** most of Europe, North Africa and the Middle East.

As the Empire grew, so did Rome: from a small town into a vast capital city. At its peak the population reached almost one million, a huge number for the time. Taxes collected from conquered peoples made Rome rich. Triumphant generals built temples and arches to celebrate their victories, while the city centre boasted many grand buildings and monuments. Shops were filled with luxury goods from across the Roman world such as gold from Spain, honey from Greece and papyrus from Egypt.

The she-wolf feeding Romulus and Remus.

HOW DID ROME GET ITS NAME? THE LEGEND OF ROMULUS AND REMUS

The god of war, Mars, had twin baby sons called Romulus and Remus. They were left to drown in a basket on the banks of the River Tiber but a she-wolf rescued them and fed them on her milk. Later, a shepherd stumbled across the boys and brought them up as his own sons. When the twins grew into strong men they built a city on the spot where the wolf had rescued them. Sadly, they couldn't agree who would be king and quarrelled. Romulus killed his brother and called the new city after himself – Rome.

Livy, a famous Roman historian (c. 59 BC – AD 17), retold the legend of Romulus and Remus in his book *The Early History of Rome.*

HIBERNIA
BRITANNIA
North Sea
• London
ATLANTIC OCEAN
GERMANIA
BELGICA
LUGDENSIS
NABONENSIS
RHAETIA
NORICUM
GAUL
• Arles
PANNONIA
DACIA
Black Sea
LUSITANIA
HISPANIA
CORSICA
Rome
ITALIA
DALMATIA
THRACE
GALATIA
ARMENIA
BAETICA
New Carthage
SARDINIA
MACEDONIA
MESOPOTAMIA
Euphrates
Tigris
MAURITANIA
SICILIA
Syracuse
Carthage
Mediterranean Sea
Athens
ACHAEA
ASIA MINOR
SYRIA
CYPRUS
NUMIDIA
CRETE
AFRICA
CYRENAICA
EGYPT
Alexandria
ARABIA

Roman Empire AD 117

This map shows the Roman Empire around the year 130 BC. Everyone in the Roman Empire was governed by Roman laws.

A model of Ancient Rome. Can you see the race-track to the left of this picture? It was used for chariot races.

🐾 The large round building in the photograph is called the Colosseum. It was built by the **Emperor** Vespasian and his sons, and opened in AD 80. What do you think it was used for?

DETECTIVE WORK
The map on this page shows the Roman names for the countries inside the Empire. Use an atlas to find the modern names of the countries the Romans once ruled.

2. What was Celtic Britain like before the Romans?

When the Romans invaded Britain the native people were called Celts. Celts also lived in the countries we now know as France, Belgium and Switzerland. British Celts lived in different tribes such as the **Iceni** in East Anglia or the Dumnonii in the West Country. Each tribe had its own ruler. Usually this was a king but under Celtic law a woman could become queen. In AD 60, for example, the Brigantes, a tribe in the north of England, were led by Queen Cartimandua.

The Romans fought against Celtic peoples for over 500 years and thought they were barbarians. Roman historians described them as 'blue painted with only one redeeming feature – bravery'. Modern **archaeologists** have found evidence such as the presence of fine Celtic jewellery to show that the Celts were not **barbarians** and that in some things, like farming, they were more skilled than the Romans.

This map shows where the different Celtic tribes lived. The Romans were able to bribe some of the tribes to help them when they invaded.

DETECTIVE WORK

Find where you live on the map. Which tribe would you have belonged to? Find out if there are any places near you with Celtic names like the river Avon, the Pennine mountains or the City of London. *The Oxford Dictionary of Place Names* is a great place to start.

Celtic men wore trousers, a short linen tunic and a long woollen cloak. Women wore tight-waisted bell shaped skirts. Shoes were made of leather or linen.

The Celts lived in round huts with walls made from wattle (woven branches) and daub (clay and mud cement). Celtic farmers were the first in Britain to protect the fertility of the fields. They sowed their crops and spread them with manure each year, instead of clearing new land when the soil was exhausted. Even the Romans admitted the Celts had better ploughs, sturdily built, with iron blades to turn heavy soils. Their diet was good too and included plenty of meat and fish. A favourite Celtic dish was salmon baked with honey and herbs.

Celtic craftsmen were highly skilled. Their metal workers made iron weapons like helmets and long swords but also decorative jewellery such as gold and silver torcs, or neck rings. Spinners, weavers and dyers, often women, made clothes of such quality and colour, that British woollen cloaks became famous across the Roman world. Celtic boat builders were so good that the Romans used the skills of the Celtic people they had already **conquered** in **Gaul** to build the transport for the fleets that invaded Britain.

☙ Look at the photograph of Maiden Castle built by the Durotriges tribe. How many sets of walls does it have? Why do you think they built so many?

Celtic tribes were warlike and often fought against each other. To defend themselves they built hill-forts with massive earth banks topped with walls or wooden stakes. This hill-fort in Dorset is called Maiden Castle.

3. Why did the Romans invade Britain?

The Celts were brave warriors and skilled charioteers. They looked terrifying and often fought without armour, their bodies painted with dye. Celtic armies fought like mobs and it was hard for their leaders to give them orders when a battle had begun.

✿ Why do you think Caesar wrote about the great difficulties his troops faced when he raided Britain?

Julius Caesar was an ambitious general and politician who was scheming to rule Rome. In 55 BC, Caesar raided Britain with an army of two **legions**. He had recently beaten the Celts in **Gaul** and was angry that the British had been helping their kinsmen to fight him. But he had other motives too. He wanted to make his name so he could become the most powerful politician in Rome.

Caesar's Raid, 55 BC:

*The Romans opened fire from their ships with bows, slings and catapults. The natives backed off a little, but still the soldiers hesitated. Then the **Standard Bearer** of the Tenth **Legion** took action. He prayed to the gods for luck and cried out in a loud voice, 'Jump down comrades, unless you want to lose the Eagle to the enemy'. Ignoring the danger he leaped into the sea towards the British. Instantly the soldiers sprang after him. They could not face the shame of losing a Roman Eagle.*

Julius Caesar wrote this account in his autobiography, *The Conquest of Gaul*, only a few years after the attack on Britain took place. The eagle was the sacred symbol of the legion.

Caesar's invasion was almost a disaster. The British were waiting on the landing beaches and at first his troops were afraid to leave their boats. After a bloody battle, the Romans won but Caesar had to return to Gaul after a storm wrecked his ships. The next year, 54 BC, he tried again with a fleet of 800 ships and nearly 40,000 soldiers. This time he defeated the Celtic war leader Cassivellaunus and left with **hostages** and plunder.

It was almost 90 years before the Romans came back to Britain. In AD 43, Rome had a new **Emperor**, Claudius, who needed to prove himself to his generals, or risk being overthrown. The conquest of Britain, he decided, was the perfect way to be seen as a great leader. Conveniently, the British had already given him an excuse to attack. The tribes of southern Britain had been fighting among themselves: King Verica, an **ally** of Rome, had been driven from his kingdom. Verica, who ruled part of Sussex, appealed to Claudius for help. The Emperor was eager to send General Aulus Plautius and an army of 40,000 men to Verica's aid.

A set of Iron Age coins, including a silver coin of the **Iceni** tribe in the top row. As well as wanting to prove himself to his generals, Claudius had another reason to invade. He believed coins like these proved **Britain** was an island rich with silver mines and pearls.

Roman soldiers were highly trained and well organised. They were divided into legions of about 5,500 legionaries. A legionary could march 30 miles a day while carrying all his kit. This included a pickaxe, saw, bucket, cooking pots and food – as well as weapons and armour.

DETECTIVE WORK

Use the Internet to find out about Claudius. What disabilities did he have and how did they make life harder for him?

4. Who were Caratacus and Boudicca?

Caratacus, King of the Catuvellauni, and Boudicca, Queen of the **Iceni**, were heroic British chiefs who fought against Roman rule. Caratacus gave battle first, during the summer of AD 43. When General Plautius, the Roman commander, landed his troops in Kent, Caratacus tried to stop them crossing the River Medway. During the day the Romans were held back, but the Celts were defeated by a surprise night attack. Soon south-east England was **conquered** and it was safe for Claudius to visit. Eleven British kings surrendered to the **Emperor** at Colchester, the capital of the new Roman province of Britannia.

One reason the Romans won so quickly was that the Celts were divided. Some kings, like Cogidubnus, welcomed the invaders and were allowed to keep their lands while others fought on. Caratacus retreated to Wales and, according to the Roman historian Tactitus, 'was joined by all those who feared Roman rule'. In AD 51, he took on the Romans again in a battle fought in the Severn Valley, but once more the **legions** proved unstoppable. Now running for his life, Caratacus fled to the lands of the Brigantes in the north of England only to be handed over to the enemy by Queen Catimandua.

This map shows the Roman invasion and the main stages of the conquest of Britain.

❧ Look at the map. Which part of Britain was never conquered by the Romans?

The biggest British revolt came a few years later, in AD 60. King Prasutagus of the Iceni tribe died and the Romans arrogantly seized his lands. Nobles were thrown out of their homes and King Prasutagus's wife, Queen Boudicca, was flogged like a slave. Faced with this outrage the Iceni and their neighbours rose up in a grim rebellion. Led by Boudicca they wiped out the Roman colony at Colchester and burned London.

The Roman governor, Suetonius Paulinus, was caught unawares. He was busy fighting a war in Wales and most of the Roman army was with him. He hurried back to fight the rebels in a desperate battle. About 80,000 Celts were killed and Boudicca poisoned herself rather than being taken prisoner after the defeat.

DETECTIVE WORK

The Roman writer Dio Cassius wrote a description of Boudicca in AD 210. He began: *'She was very tall and terrifying to look at. Her eyes flashed fiercely and her voice was harsh'.* Find the rest of his account on the Internet and draw a portrait of her.

Skulls found in the Walbrook stream in London. Archaeologists think they may have been victims of Boudicca's army.

I was whipped by the Romans when they tried to take our lands – and now I am fighting for my freedom. Think how many of us are fighting and why. We must win this battle or die. Let men live as slaves if they want. I will not.

Boudicca's speech to her army before her last battle. Written in AD 210 by the Roman historian Dio Cassius.

5. Why did the Romans build Hadrian's Wall?

In the years after Claudius, Roman **Emperors** realised that the **Empire** could not go on growing forever. There was a need to mark out the borders and make them safe against attacks from **barbarian** tribes. When the Emperor Hadrian visited Britain in AD 122 he decided to set up a northern frontier. This was to be a mighty wall stretching from the River Tyne in the East to the Solway Firth in the West (see map on page 15).

Hadrian's Wall was largely planned and built by three Roman **legions**, the II, VI and XX. Many of the men were skilled craftsmen such as masons, blacksmiths and carpenters, while some officers were experienced architects and engineers. When they were not fighting, Roman soldiers often worked on big construction projects like forts, **aqueducts** and bridges.

✿ How good are you at Roman numerals? What are the modern numbers of the legions that built Hadrian's Wall?

> *When the barbarians had been driven back and Britain had recovered, Hadrian ordered work on a wall which was to be 80 miles long, to divide the Romans from the barbarians.*
>
> Roman writer Aelius Spartianus, writing in about AD 390.

Today, Hadrian's Wall is a popular tourist destination. Thousands of people walk the wall every year.

Surveying and building the wall took 12 years. It was 118 kilometres long, 2 to 3 metres high and up to 7 metres wide. Originally painted white to stand out, it snaked across the country, always commanding the high ground. At every mile there was a small fort called a milecastle and in between were two **signal turrets.**

Hadrian's Wall was not meant to stop people travelling in and out of Roman territory, but to control them. If there was an attack, messages could be sent quickly along the wall – or to forts behind – by runners or by **semaphore.** The soldiers who manned the wall were not the legionaries who built it, they were auxiliaries (support troops) from all over the Empire: **Gaul**, Spain, Germany – and as faraway as Syria. Many of them married native girls and settled down in nearby towns. Often their sons served on the Wall after them.

The bath house at Chester's fort. Hadrian's Wall could be a cold and uncomfortable posting for a soldier. A warm bath house would have been a good place to relax.

road   vallum

wall

north ditch

A cross-section of Hadrian's Wall. In front of the wall was a ditch 3 metres deep. Behind was the vallum, a flat bottomed ditch, to keep civilians away.

6. Why did the Romans build roads?

There were no roads as we think of them in Britain before the Romans came. The Celts used ancient tracks some of which were paved, but in wet weather or winter most were impassable. Soon after the invasion, the Roman army began to build a network of brilliantly engineered, all-weather, roads. Using these roads, soldiers could march quickly from fort to fort – or to a trouble spot, such as Hadrian's Wall. Once made, the roads became important for trade with merchants moving their goods from town to town in heavy ox-carts, the goods lorries of the ancient world.

A carving showing an ox-cart. They carried goods like wine, wheat or fine pottery.

*Surveyors came to mark out
The line of the road. After them
Came diggers, packing firm
The trench to stop the road sinking
Or the soil from shifting under the pavement.
Then, the laying of kerbs,
The mating of block with block.*

*The gangs are busy
Stripping nearby hills of timber,
Making the wooden ties and smoothing in
Lumps of masonry; between each block
Mortar to bind it and fire-dried sand.*

Statius, a Roman poet, describing a new road near Rome in about AD 80. The remains of Roman roads in Britain show that the same building methods were used.

A cross-section showing Roman methods of road building on soft and firm ground.

This map shows the most important roads in Britain, about AD 150. Can you find the Fosse Way?

The standard of Roman roads was very high. Firstly, **surveyors** planned the route, then the soldiers set to work. They cut deep drainage ditches on both sides of the line of the road, about 10 metres apart. Next, a foundation of clay, gravel or local stone, like chalk, was laid. Finally, the surface of cement and paving stones was rammed into place with stout timbers. On boggy ground the soldiers laid a framework of timber piles or brushwood to stop the road sinking.

Roman roads were usually very straight. As conquerors they had no need to worry about who owned the land. Unlike today's road planners, they simply went from place to place by the most direct route. Roads built in Britain were part of a wider network of at least 70,000 kilometres of highways knitting the Empire together. A message sent from Rome by the *cursus publicus*, the imperial post, could arrive at Hadrian's Wall in just two weeks. Messengers changed horses every 10 miles and could travel 135 kilometres a day.

🐾 What does the map tell us about Roman control of Britain?

DETECTIVE WORK

One of the longest and straightest roads in Britain is the Fosse Way. Use a library encyclopaedia or Internet search to find out about the history of this road. How much of it is still in use and what modern names does it have?

Inchtuthill
Edinburgh
Hadrian's Wall
Carlisle
York
Chester
Lincoln
Wroxeter
Leicester
Caister
Fosse Way
Colchester
Caerleon
Cirencester
London
Bath
Silchester
Rochester
Richborough
Winchester
Dover
Lympne
Chichester
Exeter
Dorchester

7. What was life like in a Roman town?

The Celts had hill-forts where they would gather in times of danger, but there were no Celtic towns. The Romans, however, believed that civilised life meant town life. To encourage the British to live like Romans they built model towns, such as St Albans and Canterbury, for them to copy. These settlements were based on army forts, with a town wall and neat streets laid out in a grid pattern.

Most Roman towns had the same features. At the main crossroads in the centre was the forum. This was a market square with shops along three sides and the basilica on the fourth. The basilica was the heart of Roman power. This was a large hall where the town council met, people paid their taxes and law courts were held. In serious trials suspects and witnesses could be whipped to make them give information.

This **aerial** photograph shows the remains of the Roman theatre at St Albans in Hertfordshire.

The forum would bustle with shoppers, especially on market days. Roman shops sold many different goods including bread, fish, clothes, shoes, jewellery and weapons.

🐾 What do you think the shop in this Roman carving is selling?

It's impossible to get to sleep. You hear heavy wagons creaking through narrow streets and you're deafened by the swearing of cattle drivers whose beasts have got stuck…When you've locked up your house and brought the shutters down on your shop, and the street is still and quiet, there'll always be a burglar to rob you.

Juvenal, the famous Roman poet wrote this comic description of the problems of town life in about AD 120.

Other public buildings made town life lively. Public baths had steam rooms for sweating out dirt from your skin, but they were not just for getting clean. Bathers exercised, talked, played board games and gambled. If people were looking for excitement, the oval shaped amphitheatre was packed every holiday. Eager crowds gathered to watch wild animals fight or **gladiators** pitted against one another. Some towns, like Colchester, had a theatre where plays were put on with music and dancing. Busy inns sold food, wine and local beer while offering weary travellers a place to stable horses and sleep.

Larger towns had facilities we take for granted today. For the first time in Britain, clean water was brought in by a system of **aqueducts** and pipes, while drains and sewers were built to keep streets clean. Even so, many streets were still narrow, smelly and crowded. Ordinary people lived in simple wood-framed houses, sometimes with a shop or workshop at the front. The walls were made from wattle and daub (see page 7) but were often brightly decorated inside, perhaps with flowers or drawings of animals.

Bath houses also had public toilets. There were no cubicles and people sat together in rows, as this postcard shows. They used sponges instead of toilet paper.

DETECTIVE WORK

Try this Roman recipe for stuffed dates, with the help of an adult slave. Remove the stones from the dates and stuff them with anything you like: fruit, nuts, cake crumbs or spices. Roll them in a little salt and fry in honey.

8. What was life like in the Roman countryside?

Although towns were important for encouraging the Celts to live like Romans, only about 250,000 people in Britain (out of a population of 3 million) lived in them. Most British people barely changed their way of life during the centuries of Roman rule. They may have used Roman coins, pots and tools; they may have sold their crops in town markets, but they kept on living in thatched, round houses in small villages and farmsteads.

Some wealthy Britons, however, eagerly copied Roman ideas about farming. They built **villas**, grew new crops and lived a Roman lifestyle. The biggest villas were large and luxurious country houses like Fishbourne, near Chichester, in Sussex. This may have been the palace of Cogidubnus, a Celtic King who became a Roman citizen. Such grand villas were built of stone around a sunlit courtyard. They had central heating, piped water, hot baths, mosaic floors and wall-paintings. The remains of over 600 villas have been found in England.

Every corner is tight packed with corn. Fierce bulls roam in the valleys. The farmyard is full of geese, peacocks and partridges. Home born infant slaves collect the eggs. One farm worker brings in a huge cheese, another a basket of dormice, a third pale honey in its comb.

The Roman writer Varro describes a villa in Italy in the first century BC.

✿ Look at the quote by Varro. What do you think the Romans did with dormice?

A reconstruction of a Roman villa at Butser Ancient Farm, in Hampshire.

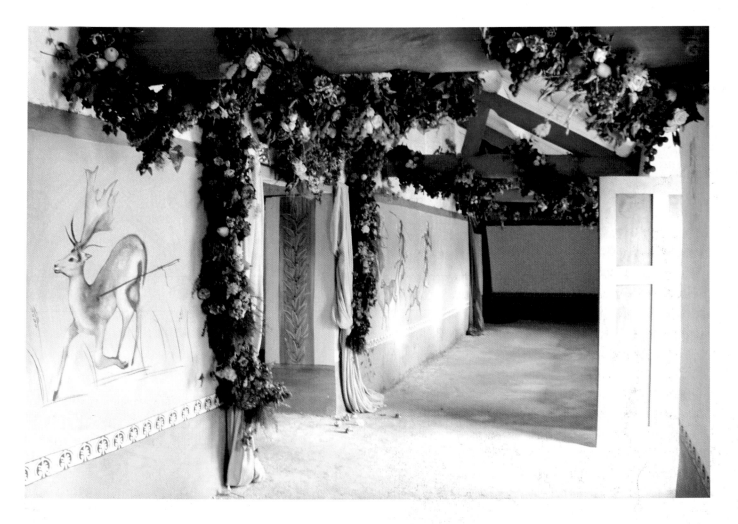

Villas were not just homes, they were the focus of bustling **estates** run to make money. Villas supplied most of the food for the army and people who lived in towns, so usually they were built near a road. To meet this demand, exciting new types of fruit and vegetables were grown for the first time: carrots, parsnips, celery, black plums, cherries, walnuts, apples, pears and even grapes. In fact, many of the foods we know today. Breeds of farm animals too, like pigs, were improved to become bigger and fatter with crops like turnips being grown for fodder to feed the animals over the winter.

Villas were home not only to the landowner and his family, but also their servants and slaves who worked the land. Slaves were the property of their masters and could be kept in chains and beaten. At a villa at Hambleden in Buckinghamshire many bodies of newborn children have been found. Historians think they were left to die – the unwanted babies of slave women.

A reconstruction of the inside of a Roman Villa. The corridor is decorated ready for a feast and the mosaic on the wall shows a hunting scene.

13. Your project

Now that it is time to think about your project, you are in for a shock. Did you know that the Romans are still with us today? They are with us because their ideas still influence the way we live. Try a piece of research on our Roman heritage. Here are a few suggestions.

Project Themes and Presentation

- Look at the photograph of the Pantheon in Rome, built on the orders of the **Emperor** Hadrian. Roman styles of architecture have been widely copied through the centuries. Are there any buildings near you with features like pillars, arches and pediments? Take photographs and make a PowerPoint presentation.

- Our calendar is based on the one worked out by Julius Caesar. Find out which months are named after Roman gods and emperors and write short biographies of them. Use books on the Romans to help you, and look out for chapter headings like 'The Roman Legacy' or 'What did the Romans do for us?'

- The Roman language was Latin. Most modern countries that were part of the Roman **Empire** use many words that come from Latin. Make a dictionary of Latin words and phrases that we use today, for example: status quo = 'things stay the same'.

- Roman ideas about town planning and sanitation still shape the towns we live in now. What facilities did Roman towns have that we still use today? Make an illustrated directory, using your home town as an example.

The Pantheon, in Rome, was built in about AD 125. Features from this building, such as arches and pillars, have been copied all over the world.

Here are a few more ideas:

● Go shopping and look for Latin brand names, like Aero and Flora.
● Compare the design of Roman and modern coins.
● Research how great artists have been influenced by Roman styles of art.

Sherlock Bones has been finding out about hunting dogs from Roman Britain. He found out that they were fast, tough and strong. This meant they were valuable and sold all over the Empire. The Romans liked them so much, that sometimes, they sacrificed them to the gods – or put them in arenas to fight lions or bears. Today's wolfhounds and mastiffs are their descendants.

Roman hunting dogs looked like this modern wolfhound.

Glossary

AD The years after Christ's birth.
aerial photograph A photo taken from a plane. This is one of the best ways for archaeologists to spot evidence of Roman buildings.
ally A friend.
aqueducts Raised channels, sometimes as big as bridges, carrying water over long distances.
archaeologists People who study remains from ancient times.
barbarians A Roman word for uncivilised people.
BC The years before Christ's birth.
civil wars Wars between people in the same country, not against outside enemies.
conquered To be defeated and taken over.
decompose To rot away.

emperor The ruler of an empire. The first Roman Emperor was called Augustus.
empire A country or state which rules over a number of other countries.
epitaph Words carved on a tomb.
estates Large farms.
Gaul The Roman province that covered France, Belgium and the Rhine region of Germany.
gladiators A specially trained warrior fighting to entertain the crowds. Sometimes they fought to the death.
hostages Prisoners who are held to guarantee the good behaviour of their people.
Iceni A tribe in East Anglia.
legion A Roman army unit with about 5,500 men.

merchants People who made a living by buying and selling things.
organic material Items that are made from things that were once alive, like leather from cattle skin.
prophecy To tell the future.
resistance A group of people who wanted to throw the Romans out of power.
seamstress A woman who makes a living by sewing.
semaphore A system of sending messages by flags or flashes of light from lanterns.
signal turret A watch tower.
standard bearer The soldier who carried the sacred symbol of the legion: an eagle on a pole.
surveyors A person who planned engineering projects, like the route of a road.
villa A country house.

Further Information

Books to read
Britain in Roman Times by Tim Locke (Franklin Watts, 2008)

The Romans: Reconstructed by Jason Hook (Wayland, 2007)

On the Trail of the Romans in Britain by Richard Wood (Franklin Watts, 2000)

Men, Women and Children in Ancient Rome by Jane Bingham (Wayland, 2007)

Websites
Take a look at the Museum of Antiquities website:
http://museums.ncl.ac.uk/archive/index.html

Take an interactive tour of Roman Colchester at:
www.colchestermuseums.org.uk

The Romans in Britain is a huge website packed with information. Go on line at:
www.romans-in-britain.org.uk

The website addresses (URLs) included in this book were valid at the time of going to press. However, because of the nature of the Internet, it is possible that some addresses may have changed, or sites may have changed or closed down since publication. While the author and publisher regret any inconvenience this may cause the readers, no responsibility for any such changes can be accepted by either the author or the publisher.

Answers

Places to visit

Hadrian's Wall has many places to visit. Two of the best are Segedunum Fort at Wallsend near Newcastle and Housesteads Fort, six miles from Haltwhistle.

Visit the reconstructed Roman villa and Iron Age farm at Butser Ancient Farm near Petersfield, Hampshire. (www.butser.org.uk)

See the remains of brilliant first century mosaics at Fishbourne Roman Palace Chichester, West Sussex. (www.sussexpast.co.uk/fishbourne/)

Many museums have excellent Roman finds. A good one is Verulamium Museum, St Albans, Hertfordshire. (www.stalbansmuseums.org.uk)

Page 5 ❀ Games such as fights between gladiators or wild animals.

Page 7 ❀ Three sets of walls. If attackers broke through one set they would face an even higher set of walls in front of them.

Page 8 ❀ To make his victories over the British seem all the greater. As if to say 'look at all the problems my army faced, but I still won'.

Page 10 ❀ Northern Scotland.

Page 12 ❀ The Second, Sixth and Twentieth.

Page 15 ❀ There are few roads in Wales and Scotland, showing the Romans never fully controlled them.

Page 16 ❀ This shows a butcher cutting a joint of meat. Other cuts of meat are hanging from the ceiling.

Page 18 ❀ They ate them. Stuffed dormice were a Roman delicacy.

Page 20 ❀ To say thank you to the gods when their injured arm healed. Sometimes models were left when someone was still sick to remind the god which body part to heal.

Page 22 ❀ She is lying on a couch surrounded by her family. She is drinking from a cup and there is food on the small table in front of her. These features show she is from a wealthy family.

Page 23 ❀ Liberta means a freed slave – she was given her liberty.

Page 25 ❀ The castle and church were built in the Middle Ages. The walls are Roman. Why let a perfectly good set of Roman walls go to waste?

Page 26 ❀ The vase shows a chariot race.

Index